W9-AOZ-012

Kangaroos

Kate Riggs

CREATIVE EDUCATION • CREATIVE PAPERBACKS

Published by Creative Education and Creative Paperbacks
P.O. Box 227, Mankato, Minnesota 56002
Creative Education and Creative Paperbacks
are imprints of The Creative Company
www.thecreativecompany.us

Design by Ellen Huber; production by Joe Kahnke
Art direction by Rita Marshall
Printed in the United States of America

Photographs by Corbis (John Carnemolla, Sebastian
Kennerknecht/Minden Pictures, Otto Rogge), Dreamstime
(Anankkml, Nancy Dressel, Iakov Filimonov, Isselee,
Kazzadev, Odua, Ovydyborets, Renzzo, Gianna
Stadelmyer), Getty Images (Auscape), iStockphoto (GlobalP,
JohnCarnemolla, mastersky, ross1248, Smileus), National
Geographic Creative (MITSUAKI IWAGO/MINDEN PICTURES)

Library of Congress Cataloging-in-Publication Data
Riggs, Kate.
Kangaroos / Kate Riggs.
p. cm. — (Seedlings)
Includes bibliographical references and index.
Summary: A kindergarten-level introduction to kangaroos,
covering their growth process, behaviors, their home in
Australia, and such defining features as their big back feet.
ISBN 978-1-60818-739-3 (hardcover)
ISBN 978-1-62832-335-1 (pbk)
ISBN 978-1-56660-774-2 (eBook)
1. Kangaroos—Juvenile literature.
QL737.M35 R54 2016
599.2/22—dc23   2015041985
CCSS: RI.K.1, 2, 3, 4, 5, 6, 7;
RI.1.1, 2, 3, 4, 5, 6, 7; RF.K.1, 3; RF.1.1

First Edition HC 9 8 7 6 5 4 3 2 1
First Edition PBK 9 8 7 6 5 4 3 2 1

TABLE OF CONTENTS

Hello, kangaroos!

Six kinds of kangaroos live in Australia. Two kinds are called wallaroos.

Long-tailed kangaroos
have thick fur.

Some kangaroos are red.
Others are gray.

Kangaroos jump on their big back feet.

Sometimes they box with them!

Kangaroos eat grass and leaves. They eat woody plants, too.

Baby kangaroos are called joeys. They grow in a pouch. Joeys drink milk at first. Then they eat grass.

Groups of kangaroos
live together. They
rest in the shade. They
watch for danger.

All the kangaroos jump away!

Goodbye, kangaroos!

Picture a Kangaroo

ears

eye

snout

paw

claw

pouch

20

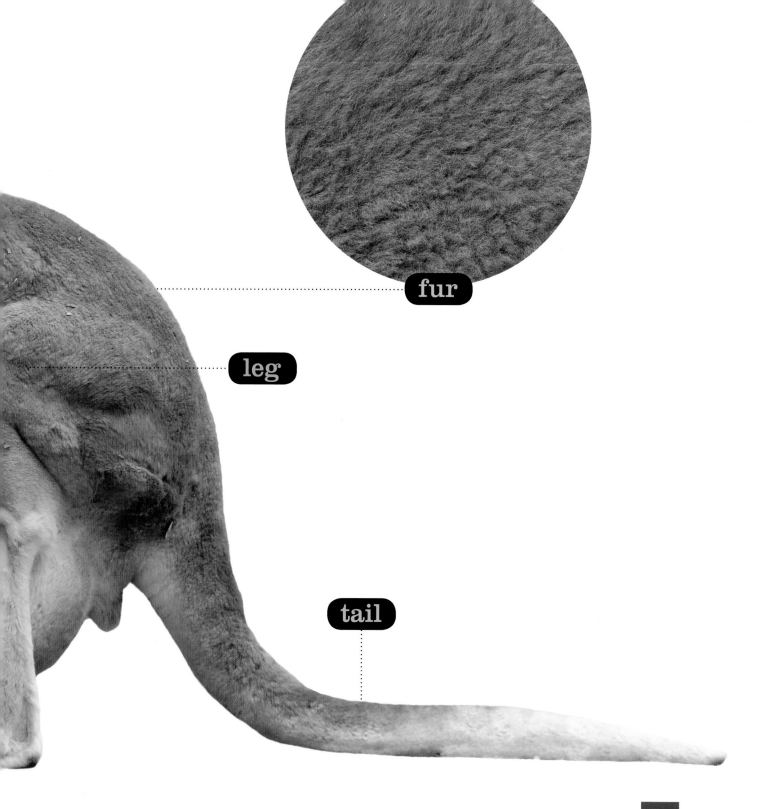

fur

leg

tail

fur: the short, hairy coat of an animal

pouch: a pocket on the stomach of a female kangaroo

Read More

Meister, Cari. *Do You Really Want to Meet a Kangaroo?*
Mankato, Minn.: Amicus, 2016.

Schuetz, Kari. *Kangaroos.*
Minneapolis: Bellwether Media, 2013.

Websites

Kangaroo Crafts for Kids
http://www.artistshelpingchildren.org
/kangarooscraftsideasactivitieskids.html
Print out examples to make your own kangaroo crafts.

National Geographic Kids: Coloring Book
http://kids.nationalgeographic.com/explore/nature
/coloring-book-animals-j-to-z/
Find a picture of a red kangaroo to color.

Index